Honest Reflections

For Everyday Life

By
Traei Tsai

Acknowledgement

I want to acknowledge that the land on which I live and work is the traditional and unceded territory of the Kwikwetlem Nation and lies within the shared traditional territories of the Tsleil-Waututh, Katzie, Musqueam, Squamish, Quay Quayt and Sto:lo First Nations.

CONTENTS

"Honesty and transparency make you vulnerable. Be honest and transparent anyway."

- Mother Theresa -

This is a modern-day book of honest reflections with photos and artwork I have taken and created over the span of three decades. Photographs from pre-smart phone, pre-apple iphone time periods and from traditional camera devices, genuinely capturing what I saw that day, in that precise moment. Abbas Kiarostami, an Iranian film director, screenwriter, poet, photographer, and film producer, observed that photography is something that captures what we are not seeing. He says, "I've often noticed that we are not able to look at what we have in front of us, unless it's inside a frame. I am a tree that is rooted in the ground." Did words come first for reflection or is it the images that we see? Kiarostami said that "in the beginning was the word, but for me the beginning is always an image." For each image in this this book, they are accompanied by a complementary honest reflection to provide you with a glimpse into your own reality. The very awareness that can happen daily to each and every one of us. It lets you stop and reflect about similar circumstances and situations in your life. Study each photo and explore the where, what, when, how, and why of each. What are you feeling? Do they resonate with your life and journey?

This book has been written to capture traces of daily life. While you will find traces of these reflections in your daily life, it may help bring to lightness, understanding, and healing to all the hardships, love, relationships, life events that have occurred that is sometimes just beyond ones control. As John Lennon sang in his song "Beautiful Boy (Darling Boy)," "Life is what happens to you while you're busy making other plans." Are you curious what this song sounds like? Stop and take a moment and listen to the song. Fulfill your curiosity, go search for it and let the unknown be known. Leave no stone unturned so they do not remain just random pebbles of life. John Lennon wrote it for his son, Sean. Life really does happen while you are doing something else. While living your life and doing something else, these depictions of my reflection will help you connect with yourself and perhaps others as well. Read one reflection then pause and ponder. You have the freedom to make notes and write out your thoughts. Study the photo and read the next reflection. You can come back to the book at any time. The photos and words are the wonders of self-exploration, permitting you the space to ponder.

I am dedicating this book all those people that truly and genuinely provided guidance and support through each stage of this journey. This book has been in the making since 2002 and I want to thank MK for the reinvigoration in noticing the daily mundane tasks in life indeed has many layers of meanings. There are also people that I may know personally as well as strangers that I have met where they have each help influenced and shaped this journey. Some are reflections that have been triggered as I listened to other people's narratives which were not my own but provoked further deep thoughts. My dedication also includes you, the reader, in finding your way to this book. May these timeless and modern reflections challenge and empower your core while awakening your frame of mind on life with honesty, clarity, frankness, empathy, humility, and all with a sense of irony.

"It's not where you start, but where you stand"

Photographed: April 7th, 2012
Location: Vancouver, BC at 9:33 pm

A reflection of…
(From Oxford Languages)

hon·es·ty
/ˈänəstē/
 The quality of being honest.

clar·i·ty
/ˈklerədē/
The quality of transparency or purity.

frank·ness
/ˈfraNGknəs/
The quality of being open, honest, and direct in speech or writing.

em·pa·thy
/ˈempəTHē/
The ability to understand and share the feelings of another.

hu·mil·i·ty
/ (h) yo͞oˈmilədē/
A modest or low view of one's own importance; humbleness.

i·ro·ny
/ˈīrənē/
A state of affairs or an event that seems deliberately contrary to what
one expects and is often amusing as a result.

Introduction

This all really started 2 decades ago. As I type this you are probably wondering why you have picked up this book and what this book will unveil for you. I am not going to tell you that this book is going to change your life, but it will change your perception about life, love, family, maybe even your career. Perhaps, it will pause your presence for a moment to reflect who you truly are so that you can squirm in the discomfort of your true existence to arrive comfortably in your own skin. Remember, you can come back to any entry and read it again. Go grab a cup of coffee or tea with your pen and notebook to jot down your deep thoughts. Be honest, write freely and truthfully as if no one is watching you. They are all significant because if the reflections have even momentarily caused you to pause and reflect, then 'these reflections have served its purpose. Don't be afraid of awakening your mind and diving in, to provoke deep thoughts that have been waiting for you all this time.

"Be Yourself, Everyone Else is Already Taken"
- Oscar Wilde -

"The clouds of nothingness floats constant"

Photographed: January 21st, 2014, at 1:45 pm
Location: Caribbean Skies

Modern Hopes

All the rings we buy are about hopes.
Rings of gemstones are filled with hopes of healing, a future.
Watches of time with measurement of hearts and pulses
Mobile phones with great photo and video functions
Computers with best specs
Creams, books, food, diets, carts, art, clothes, bags, medicine, credit cards, banks, jobs, job titles, stocks, crypto, houses, travels….
Whatever you name and look
They are all hope based
We are constantly hoping
Subconsciously buying hopes 24/7
Nail polish, condoms, birth controls, medicine, drugs, TVs, game consoles, magazines, books, pens, papers, post cards, clothes
Just thinking it,
Makes it a hope
Nothing escapes this innate desire of hope
We need it.
We crave it.
We lust for it.
Our social media is laced with hope depravation
To be filled with hopes from desperation
Every post online is hoping for the validation of its audience
When hope diminishes
Like a zombie we go hunting for hopes
Even a photo from 100 years ago
Was a snapshot opportunity of hope?
Just look around you at every single item.
Even the screen saver on your computer screen is a hope.

"Le Papillon"

Photographed: July 1, 2019
Location: Washington, DC

Periods in Love

If you have been in a relationship
For almost a decade
The stability of that is learned
Once a foundation that you thought was made of concrete
Only to find out it can crack over the years
Crumbling in an instant
Where one is trapped
Paralyzed in the debris of love
Its independence mixed in with the broken concrete bits
Held back in every viable way
5 months out of a relationship of 6 years
Almost a decade
One does not know where they begin or end
The merging of 2 lives suddenly split like peas
The only other comparable pain is when your father
passed away
Tragically in an accident that you could not witness
When his skull cracked, and his brain bled out
What is the level of that pain, you asked?
Imagine and visualize that with your most traumatic event
Now multiply it by 9
Only to relate superficially
Not to be mistaken as a competition to win the category of
pain
Because no one ever needs to win a Nobel Prize in the
ranking of pain

"Chained hearts"

Photographed: August 21st, 2010, at 8:55 am
Location: On the path of Cinque Terre,
Italy

Summer of 2007
Song Recommendation: "Elegy" by Leif Vollebekk

Old friends unite on a sizzling summer evening
In their usual spot for coffee
Life is pondered over Starbucks and cigarettes
Young and full of dreams
Nothing was quite written except for the university exams
Yearning for freedom to escape our comfort zones
And things that revolt us
A blending of naiveté and wonder
Circles through the exhaling of the smoke rings
He speaks of dreams
She speaks of uncertainties
They discussed about life after graduation
With profound realization that school was a safe haven of
familiarity
He inhales his cigarette
She looks up as he described the desired desert drive
"What's that"? She asked
"Imagine driving through the desert of the Nevada Skies in
a Volkswagen convertible as the wind blows through your
hair…"
A vision of freedom in the air
Freedom in every breath we take
Unbeknownst to us this little future envisioned
A friendship with separate journeys not yet carved
Their gaze shifts to their two new breath of smoke rings
Crossing paths into an infinite 8
Nothing was more certain than all those freedom
expressions
Like the outcomes of smashed pumpkins.

"The reflection of you"

Photographed: September 27th, 2009
at 3:22 pm
Location: Driving through Oregon, WA

Our Limbos

How does one move forward when you are in a state of
limbo?
How do you get out of the rut of a good and bad routine?
A routine that you established with the norms defined by
many

Can moving forward feel like dipping your fingers in a sack
of beans?
Then, with deliberate slowness of self-sabotage
You slowly slide your fingers out
Do all our mistakes slide off like the beans?
Never sticking?

Can you ascend and descend the spiraling staircase
simultaneously?
Unsteady hands on the railing
Stepping down then up
Your mind spiraling in the state of limbo
Drowned in the looping of your existence

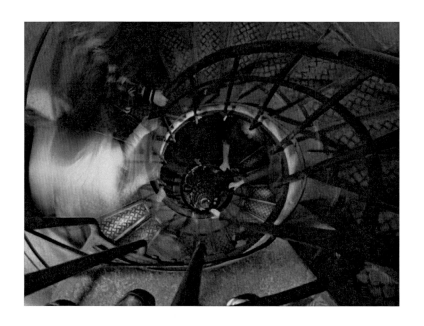

"Spirals in a state of limbo"

Photographed: September 27th, 2009
at 3:22 pm
Location: France, 2007

Holistic Anxieties

For 6 months he feared this small lump
Located under his right armpit
He suspected that it could be cancerous
The doctor advised holistic treatment
Applying tea tree oil for some weeks
It shrivelled up and went away
What would you do?

This single pore of incident confirms the constant state of
anxieties in life
Sometimes necessary, sometimes not.

Fast forward 895 days later here in mid-summer
A fortunate incident of just clogged pores
The hair trapped in the follicle
Also trying hard to find its own existence
While undergoing an existential epidermal crisis
This is undoubtedly the holistic anxieties of a clogged pore
In the light years of existence
Right here in 2020

"The Chair of Nothingness"

Photographed: A day in the month of May
Location: Vancouver, BC

1 -1-1-1

Funny that I keep seeing 1111.
11:11am, 1:11pm, and 11:11pm
Am I where I am supposed to be in life now?
Some days seem brighter than others, but some days are
so dark that even the light cannot shine through, he told
me.
"I wish I could have your life," she told me.
This young girl, of course did not know of my journey
All I could say to her was,
"Never think never because last year this time I had not a
clue that this was where I'd be

Life is strange like that.
We somehow end up doing things we never thought
possible
Or be encapsulated in situations that seemed impossible
or non-existent previously
You can say life has the amazing capacity to amaze and
shock you
Such is the beauty of life to embrace every moment

I looked into her innocent eyes
A sweet face without real trauma and heartbreak
Perhaps some are more fortunate than others
Riding through life without heartaches
Or was she any more fortunate than those that have been
heartbroken?
Will she soon be heartbroken?
How will she recover?
Will she heal the same as others?
Regardless, life always goes on.
The wounds are and will always be there.
Healing with permanent keloid scars

Like badges of trauma
The beauty of life is that it always does whatever
necessary so that one can move forward
Just think back to what you were doing exactly at this time
last year.

"Those Eyes"

Photographed: June 22, 2004
In memory of my dog that passed in January
2017.
British Columbia

Hopes

They existed frequently and constantly when we were young.
It started with the first taste of ice cream.
You longed and hoped to try it again.
Once you tried it, you hoped to try more flavors.

In elementary school, you hoped that it would be your turn next on the swings.
You hoped that you could play games with other children in your class.

Hopes are ingrained in cultural contexts
In North America, growing up you would be excited for sleepovers at your best friend's house.
In Asia, you would be excited because you get to see your friends at your tutor class after a full day of school

In high school, you had hoped that the most popular guy at school would look at you.
Not knowing that he ended up being the first guy to marry and in divorce number 2 already
While studying in university, you became lost in the hopes of what could become your future.

In a new country, you had hoped to quickly settle like locals
Not knowing that the newcomer path of integration can be filled with discrimination and bias
As you navigate, you discover and renew dead hopes to create the future you think you wanted at that moment
All the job and school applications you had sent out were filled with hopes.

Each and every single application regardless of outcome is history since the initial submission
Now, while grappling with the realization of how fast time passes
Your hopes diminish only to create more new hopes
The hopes that exist in your head are to put actions in place as there is still time to change what is yet to come

Hope will always be there because that is what pushes you to try your utmost best.

"The Endless Search for Hope"

Photographed: August 21, 2012, at 5:14 am
Location: Cinque Terre, Italy

Stereotypical Husband fees

A honest husband is likely humble and less ambitious.
He will attend to your needs over his own.
Because he allocates time for this TLC to you, to both of
you, he allocates less time in achieving success and
wealth.
Thus, this causes you to pay a fee. You will compensate
for his lack of financial capability.

A deadbeat husband spends much of his time for his own
needs. He is consumed and absorbed in himself, more
than he will ever for you. His time is allocated much to his
own life that there isn't much time to pursue anything else.
The fee that you have to pay is of time, finance, and
everything required to make up the 99.9% of this
relationship.
When there is a grain of neutral traits, you treasure it and
hold onto this 0.01% potential of possibility.

A successful husband is likely charismatic and full of
ambition. He often forgets about you and spends much of
his time acquiring more wealth, and likely pursuing instant
gratitude in objective wealth and of course other women.
Time is allocated to you when his ounce of guilt kicks in,
this same allocated amount is split with the children that
you may have together. For this relationship, your fees are
your time, your youth, your sacrifices as a doting
wife/mother, and much emotional stress, lack of sex, and
much sadness. Your best friend is a wine glass and
Prozac. Not even the most beautiful bag or jewelry can
satisfy this loneliness pit inside of you.
When you receive a gift, you immediately wonder what he
has done wrong.

A general husband is one whom that performs all husband/partner duties in a mediocre manner. Not because he is mediocre by default but rather life circumstances have not pushed him to his full potential, and it likely never will because it is enabled and nurtured by you without you realizing it. This fee that you pay is acceptance, a good chunk of your finances, time, and bearing his children, if any. Whatever he lacks or is inadequate, you will compensate to make it work because there is no other way.

"What kind of Husband Are You?

Photographed: July 16, 2022
Location: Lost in London, UK

Wants - August 29, 2018

When you want it, it never comes.
When you do not want it, they come unexpectedly.
The things that you most care about suddenly becomes
unimportant.
The rank of importance drops.
When it no longer exists, you yearn for it.
Like a vacation you took but didn't start to fully enjoy it until
your fingers flipped through all the good and terrible shots
you took on the trip.
Your heart starts full of love and expectations.
Things happen and they disappoint you.
It becomes disappointed, empty, and full of emotions in
which you cannot control. Then poof!
Just like that, it becomes restless.
All the things that your heart yearned for over the years
comes rushing back.
This cycle repeats like a train ride on a loop,
Except this time, you stop at the station called
'Restlessness'.
You get out of this stop and dance in the rhythm of
restlessness,
Realizing all the unattended longings over the years.
When each cycle runs its course,
Once again you get on the train,
To embark on this journey
Finally arriving at the final stop of detachment,
A station that is untethered.
Your heart, now empty and without longing.

It's funny how when they come, you no longer want them.
Perhaps we should just all wait those wants out for a bit
longer.

"Nothing but an empty cup left."

Photographed: November 9, 2012, at 3:31 pm
Location: Taipei, Taiwan

Old
December 14, 2018

She was old and cold drenched by the extremely chilly and heavy rainfall.
She wore a blue hooded rain jacket, a leather hobo bag and Hunter brand sneaker boots.
She seemed well dressed and had transition glasses.
I saw her as she leaned against the pole.
Her face showed her pain while the rain continued to drop onto her transition lenses.
I asked her if she was all right.
She said she wasn't feeling well at all, felt nauseous.
She muttered that she was at the Elizabeth Center for class.
I unintentionally made her repeat three times because I couldn't hear through the thick noise of the city streets and rain.

One lady stopped to inquire if she was okay after seeing I stopped. A few affluent gentlemen with silver hair in their fine long black coats turned to look over at us, under the safe covers of their expensive umbrellas.
They did not come over -   likely because someone else was taking care of it.

I asked if she wanted to get something warm, sit for a bit to warm up.
She said no because she can't eat.
I asked if there was anyone to call, her family.
She said: "I don't have any family to call".
I told her we should get out of the rain; it is too cold.
She agreed.
I picked up her two Safeway plastic bags that were heavy with food.

I scanned rapidly for a cover, saw a staircase leading underground and suggested this. She said no she didn't want to go downstairs.
I then located an outdoor table and seat with a slanted blue umbrella.

We approached for cover and rested there for 2 minutes.
On the way, she told me she had a sole fillet for lunch but barely touched her food because she was feeling ill since yesterday.
I offered again to get her something warm, perhaps a chamomile tea to ease her stomach, settle her nausea.
She said no.
She thanked me again for helping her.
We paused momentarily before I held the umbrella for her for another block.

I told her we'd stop at the next street corner.
I wanted to find her an umbrella.
When we arrived, she looked a bit better, said thank you that she really appreciated my help.
I said: "Can I get you anything, do you want a hot tea?"
She said no.
I said: "let me try to get you an umbrella..."
She said: "No, I couldn't... it be too much to carry as I have many blocks to go".
She thanked me again and suddenly gathered her strength and picked up the two bags.
She looked at me and told me she will go home now.
I told her to stop and ask for help if she is not feeling well again.

As I wished her well, I studied her face, wet with rain and her white hair plastered on the sides of her face.

The rain also washed away the dried food bits on the left corner of her mouth.
Her green, grey eyes, glistening, likely from the rain and perhaps tears of sadness.
What was her childhood dream?
Did she fulfill them?
Why did she have no family?
She used to be five years old as we all have been.

You and I are all living the same lives.
I can easily be her, she could easily be me, and you could easily be her.

Will you walk me home under your umbrella when I am old, wrinkly, in poor health...standing in my Hunter boots?
Or, will you keep walking by.
What choice will you make?
Where will life take you?

"People Come, People Go"

Photographed: December 27, 2012
Location: Streets of Taipei, Taiwan

The Art of Seeing Life Truthfully

Life is a maneuver of feelings, situations, and things.
Everything is a perception.
Who placed those perceptions in your mind and shaped
the way of how you see things?

Have you stopped to ponder, reflect, and question the
reality that is presented to you?
Do you accept the truth as is, the way it has been
presented to you?
Do you accept that it is the truth and not something that
someone else is presenting to you?

We are in truth, all actors in life.
Just being who we think we should be, how to act, what to
act on.
We go through a lifetime of hearing other people's ideas
Mistaking that as our own independent thought.

The truth is, nothing is innately organic.
Unless you are confined in one space with zero contact
with anyone since birth.
Can you guarantee that your existence has absolutely no
influence from external factors?

The eyes, emotions, experiences are never stringent.
Or, do we rinse our eyes with alcohol?

"Seeing Truthfully"

Photographed: Summer, 2021
Location: Vancouver, BC

Socks

They come in pairs only because we have two feet
Socks, thy cushion and protect our feet.
From sweat, blisters and all the steps we take daily.
10,000 steps daily, they say!
Why can't you find the way?
In all the steps we take,
Socks don't last forever
Sometimes holes appear and stains from the insides of
your shoes creates a permanent mark.
Laundering them will not remove the stains.
Expensive socks and cheap socks, they will all need to be
replaced at some point.

Take a moment, and look at your sock collection.
Where have they taken you in life?

Did you know socks are easily the most important thing to
donate but we often just donate clothes or bigger items we
have no use for?

Socks, insignificantly small but filled with dignity and
importance for the period they served their purpose in your
life.

"Gendered and phallic since the beginning."

Photographed: August 23, 2012
Location: City of Pompeii, Italy

Khisigharba Buddha's Life Taxes

Whatever you took in excess, whether in your previous or current life. Be rest assured that you will need to return this in one form or another.

The man that prostitutes his soul and seeks for the prostitute in others
Be rest assured that his beloved and most cherished will encounter similar fate.
His daughters and sons may possibly encounter the same fate from his treatment to others.

The beggar that steals from others will be sure to have his goods stolen too.

If you cannot look for the beauty in the eyes of others and speak only with kindness, be sure the universe is fair and just in that cause and effect will be delivered to you in the same manner.

Perhaps…
What taxes you choose to pay or not
Becomes the karmic life taxes yet to come.

"*Temple Tourists*"

Photographed: December 27, 2012
Location: Taipei, Taiwan

Unpaid Parking tickets

Why do they come you ask?
They come and you do not pay.
Some have no reason or rhyme, only that you were there
at the wrong time and place.
Depending on culture, perhaps it was bad karma or bad
luck.
You deserved it because of the many times you got away.
But then, it could just be a glitch in your parking app or
purely unwelcomed timing.

"The Secret in the Mirror"

Photographed: August 24th, 2010
Location: Somewhere in Monaco.

Life is like a masquerade

Why? You ask
Even as a child, you were never at ease.
Always under some sort of surveillance of a life watch.

When have you ever been at ease?
You wake up, you make the bed because someone else
told you that you should
You take a shower and check yourself out in the mirror
and see your naked self.
You look at your flaws and or admire your good features.

You then get up and get dressed.
Put on your modern masquerade mask to face the world.

Be it your work at the office.
Be it your role as a parent.
Be it your role as a partner.
Be it your role as family.

Whatever it is, even late in the evening while you hold
your mobile phone in your hands and doze off to sleep,
you are still wearing that mask, living that front stage life
of others in the very body of your back stage life.

Slowly...you drift into sleep. Awake and repeat.

"Who do you want to Be Today?"

Photographed: Summer, 2017
Location: New Orleans, USA

The Value of Nothing

The stud that fell out of the hair clip that was made in Korea.
You realized this as you bent down to pick up the glittery stud.
While holding it in your hands you realized how one can be caught up with the trivial things in life.
While you process how to repair and glue this glitter stud on, the outside world is full of joy, anger, hunger, war and temptations.

Did you know that your significant other was subject to temptation and could have done something that could not be undone?

A homeless man drifts off to sleep on the side walk and will likely never wake up the next day.

The group of people at the Parlour Lounge celebrates their 25th birthday surrounded by drunken friends, reckless with abandon of all the actions that can change their lives, or others.

An elderly woman with COVID-19 sighs her last breath and passes away at her hospital bed, surrounded by no one because she has no family.

Tears roll down the corner of a man's eyes
Once a triathlon 12 months ago
Now struggling with his last breath
Finally passing away without a family in sight
Because they cannot be near.

A baby opens its eyes for the first time

And sees his mother and father.
They smile at one another
Drenched in awe of the gift of life.

Maybe for today
Pause momentarily
and really don't sweat the small stuff.

"To Each His Own"

Photographed: August 22, 2010
Location: Streets of Naples, Italy

Photographs

If only we could go back in time
As there was a day
in its precise moment of prime
Life filled the bodies with existence
Beauty flowed with fluidity
where there was no resistance
dancing in all of life's dichotomy

The restless continues to ponder
how one can return to that second
where the future was still filled with wonder
Reality returns in which all were taken

Suddenly, the photographs transforms to sepia then black
and white.
In a blink of an eye
Life can pass you by without even a fight.

"All the Years Before"

Photographed: March 15th, 2013
Location: Family photos, Mom's House

Where to Park?

"What a shitty job!"
Jane Smith parks her vehicle in the second spot of the block.
She gets out of her vehicle and locks it with her remote.
She turns to glance at the vehicle one last time before she heads into the pharmacy to pick up the medication for her anaphylaxis.
While waiting for the medication to be prepared, she runs into her old friend whom she has not seen for 10 years.
Caught up in the reunion chatter, her energy perks up and is filled with fond memories of her high school friend.
Jane learns that her friend has twins and owns her own beauty company.
The PA announces that her medication is ready for pick up.
Mindful and in fear of her parked car
She ends the conversation quickly and pays for her medication.
When she returns to her vehicle, she realized she was 2.5 minutes overdue for her parking fees.
A glistening white slip rests confidently and securely underneath her wipers.
Great care was taken to ensure the wind does not blow it away
She looks up and sees the parking guy issuing more tickets on the block.

"What a shitty job!" she thought aloud.

"Boxed Vision"

Photographed: August 20th, 2010
Location: Nice, France

On Love

As one makes their way up the mountains of their hike,
along the path and surrounded by nature and trees,
Lovers carve their marks about their journey.
Why is there an urge to leave such mark?
Are we influenced by the poetry we have heard and seen
and is there a poet that resides in each of our hearts?

Love, what is love?
It comes in many forms.
There is never a simple type of love.
Every love has layers.
It is what makes it unique and individual.

In the moment, one says they are in love.
In the next, they are not.
When they look back, they are nostalgic of the love,
sometimes hateful of the love.
After some reflection, they feel they never loved.
Some days, they yearn for that love that exists in the
corner of their heart based on memories of the past.
Is it love?
Ask yourself is it love?
The answer is yes.
Although in contrasting times, they are and have all been
love.
Whatever form or depths.
Referring to a deep love and not of shallow existence.
Of course, there is also foolish love.
This is the love stemming from primal instincts.
Foolish because of its temporal state.
It's up to your own self to decide, what kind of love?
The fir t and foremost should always be self-love.

"Does Vincenzo love Kelly or Karolina?"

Photographed: August 21, 2010
Location: Somewhere in Cinque Terre

Audio Books

Why is it so hard to read yet it is so easy to read?
Gone are the days where there are no audio books.
Today, you plug the 3mm ac jack into your smartphones or
turn on blue tooth to connect with your wireless headset.
Voila!
You are 'reading' by 'listening.'
How easy it is to accomplish this task of enjoying
Perhaps this is what is called inspiration.
If only life can be this easy.
You just plug in or turn up the volume and all the wisdom
and lessons are played out to you to master immediately
You can even bookmark precisely the second and come
back to the same spot.
What if life was like an audio book?
You can play, pause, resume, skip ahead, and also go
back to a specific point in that subject?

The audio control of life does not exist.

Since birth, our life has been on a permanent auto-play.
A button that is broken because it never stops.
At times, events in life may seem like a pause or perhaps a
complete halt, like a strong press of the 'STOP' button.
Yes, with that much force.
It then appears to resume, when you decide to continue
with what the universe has prepared for you.
They say the universe never gives you more than what you
can handle.
Only…there was never a pause because life has always
been on autopilot until death greets.
Coming to a catapulting *halt!*
And just like that, life lands and ends in the very same dirt
where all seeds always sprout again.

"Be Present"

Photographed: February 6, 2018
Location: Vancouver, BC

Work

Day in and out we go to work.
When we are young, we are told to study hard.
As teens, we learn about ourselves and study as we
progress in life.
After high school, we are still studying, hoping to hone and
shape our potential future career.
When we leave school, we hope to find a job.
When we start working, we realize a thing or two, that this
job may be suitable or not for me.
We then repeat and search for new work if the
circumstances permit.
Sometimes, we are not so lucky to have work and
sometimes luck is on our side.
One is never content.
We grow tired of the very work we do daily
Perhaps also lose the meaning of why we do the work that
we do.
Why do you work?
What is your work's purpose?
Is your life meaningful because of your work or do you
create meaningful work because you have work?
Or do you work so that you can have choices in life?

"Choices?"

Photographed: July 14, 2017
Location: London, UK

A Piece of Paper

Blank at birth and awaiting to be filled.
You pick up a pen and the strokes appear as the tip of your
pen inks it.
Alphabets of your language fill the page and a story
unfolds.
You put down the pen and pick up a brush.
A fresh piece of paper this time,
You dip your paint brush into the ultramarine blue oil paint,
Feathers it across the page with satisfaction.
The beauty lies in the blankness of this piece of paper.
You can, literally place anything on it.
Or get a new sheet.

WHAT ARE YOU LEAVING BEHIND?

"What are you leaving behind?

Sketched: July 3rd, 2022
Location: Vancouver, BC

Paper bags

Where possible, stores now insist on environmentally friendly bags.
If you think about it, cheaply made bags whether it costs 35 cents or free of charge, will rip right through without having to travel too far.
A well made one, even if with Kraft paper and handles placed proportionately will perhaps carry your groceries twice or more.
Therefore, sometimes it is about the state of quality.
For all the moments we lived care-free
The cost of that lies in the paper bag Band-Aids
How much have you invested in your efforts to protect the environment in all the things you do?
Is your life like the cheap and fragile paper bag or the high quality paper bag?
Or, is it like a reusable bag?
Do you have a paper bag Band-Aid tape in life?
Why and what do you use it for?

"Matched Affair"

Photographed: November 9, 2010
Location: A corner in Taipei, Taiwan

Reading

Reading is considered a quality time.
People romanticize the idea of holding a physical copy of a
book and pouring over the pages
Eagerly absorbing the words on the pages.
You look up for a moment, pondering what else may the
sentence mean?
You then resume where you left off.
Perhaps your eyes become tired, and you doze off.
There are two experiences of reading: alone in solitude or
reading together with your partner.
A doting quality of comfort in hearing the voice of your
loved one reciting the words of the book to you.

"Be Your Own Reader"

Photographed: May 25th, 2022
Location: Somewhere in Paris, France

Labels

A symbolic definition and representation of a country is
what a flag stands for.
No one has stopped to ask why their country's flag colors
or logo were chosen.
Do you know why your flag consists of the colors it has?
What does it represent?
Some are perhaps straight forward, and some are not.
Outliers exist perhaps, but there is apparently only one flag
per country, not more than one.
It is a symbolic representation of people of one nation.
It should never be tempered with as there is much good
will associated with it (or not, depending on perceptions
and locations).
Nike's Swoosh logo is worth about $26 billions of dollars,
the most recognized brand logo in the world.
A flag on its own.
What color is your own personal flag and how much is it
worth to you not just in dollars and cents?

"A Window of Existence"

Photographed: August 24, 2010
Location: A window in Rome, Italy

Breath

Stop right where you are and take a deep breath, hold it.
Blow out that breath now.
This same breath is capable of many things.
It can blow away dust.
It can blow out air to cool the temperature source before
you to lovingly feed the spoonful of hot soup to your child.
It can create steam on a windowpane so you can draw
your happy face on it.
It can breathe life to resuscitate the near death back to life
It can also blow a flame out, or spread fire.
It can bring light and darkness.

Have you stopped to connect with your breath?
What do you notice?
The significance of breath can give life and also be a
marker for the end of life.
Whatever you do every day,
Always breathe astutely and genuinely.
Then, sleep soundly every night.

"Nature's Breath"

Photographed: August 2019
Location: Sunflower Field

Rose Quartz

Pink in its color,
Many cultures and interpretations will agree
This is a beautiful and lovely pink gemstone.
A stone of love.
With a hardness level of 7, suitable for daily wear with
care.
A pink quartz that brings love for oneself & others.
This certainly is a stone quartz that every one of us should
have.
The beauty is that there is no discrimination when it comes
to a stone for and of love.

Yet, why are there still different grades and qualities of the
stone?

"*Sparkling Heart of LiAlSi$_2$O$_6$*"

Photographed: August 2018
Location: Earth

Languages

There are about 6,500 spoken languages around the globe
from 195 countries in the world.
The most popular spoken language is mandarin Chinese.
The phonetic sounds of the language help us communicate
with one another daily.
It creates clarity and sometimes great misunderstanding.
Sometimes there are confusions because of all that is lost
in translation.
Knowledge and confidence of the spoken language affects
the delivery of your communication.

Yet, at the end of the day,
Language is an intelligent vocal deafness.
Language can transmit a message
But ingenuity and sincerity cannot be expressed even if
you speak the same language.
Our imagination holds the power to assemble the elements
of being
Translating it into the present living,
Where we are at the end of day, all the same human
beings.

"He Said, She Said, We Said, They Said"

Photographed: August 19, 2010
Location: Hidden Beach, Italy

Modern Day Hand(s)

What was the last item that you held in your hands?
Look at your fingers, feel each finger.
Look at your nails, touch each nail.
Look at the dirt underneath those nails, and think about
where it came from?
How long has it been living there?
What does your finger smell like?
The sterility of hands requires constant washing to prevent
the spread of germs and disease.

Yet it is beyond just that.
When you extend your hand, the other person can shake
your hands.
You may encounter cold hands and or warm hands.
The strength of a handshake can also tell you something
about the other person.
Sometimes, handshakes can be rejected because of
cultural taboo.

Hands in itself, have their own language of expression, not
just of ASL.
A beautiful piece of jewelry,
A ring as a symbolic companion to the hand.
They may sit wrapped closely to your Vena Amoris,
The vein to your heart in which a commitment is
intertwined.

Hands are used for cooking, washing, cleaning.
Hands are used for typing, writing, and working.
Hands are used for applying makeup, styling your hair, and
for dressing.
Hands are used for creating music, playing music, and
conducting music.

Hands are used for holding cameras for photography and for filming stories that may just last forever depending on which megapixel and all the 4Ks and 8Ks that apply.
Hands are used for changing diapers, chivalrous gestures of opening doors, and lifting heavy items.
Hands are lovely when holding your loved ones' hands as you caress it with love.
Hands are for giving pleasure.

Yet, life can be so cruel sometimes, but your hands will help uplift you.

Unisex tip: To keep them soft, you need to exfoliate and moisturize.
You can decorate your hands with art from Henna or by painting your nails.

Hands can pick up paint brushes and paint a picture with meaningful depth or nothingness for the one who works with both their hands, minds, heart, and soul is a…true artist.

But never forget that the best hands are the ones that extends to themselves.
Most importantly when those same hands extend toward others.
Sit with appreciation and gratitude and look at your hands now.
When was the last time you really admired your hands?

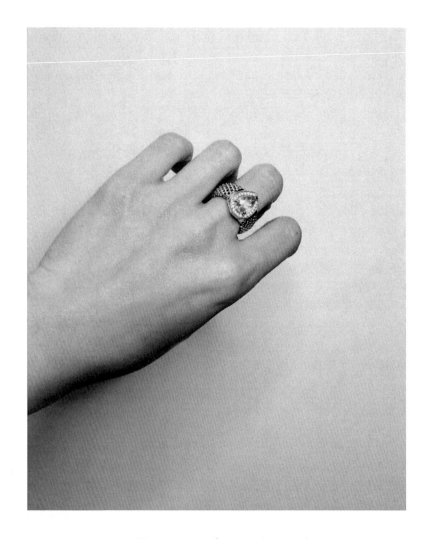

"This is Your Hand"

Photographed: October 22nd, 2019
Location: Vancouver BC

Mind Orgasms

No, not from drug induced but one that is stimulated and produced by pure intellectuality.
This is where the quantum in the physics connect on that linear line in the universe.
This form of connection,
Occurs perhaps once in a lifetime.
Maybe twice but never replicated.
They open you up to new experiences and create new experiences from the old.
They push and bring you perspectives from different angles you never thought possible.
This mind orgasm can only take place when you meet your destined significant other.
Have you had this connection?
The constant linking of the untethered and tethered connection.

"Belonging"

Photographed: August 19, 2010
Location: France

We Humans are Bastards of Honey

For millions of years, we humans are bastards.
Stealing always from the honeybees.
Robbing them continuously.
Flapping their wings at 12,000 times per minute to gather
honey for our consumption.
You asked where they went?
This is why they left and went into hiding.
At the brink of colony collapse, our daily stress is their life's
duress.
Drop, drop, drop.
Not drops of honey but bodies of our delicate bees.
Even if the honey is diluted, honey adulteration is occurring
everywhere.
Such as modern-day life, everything has a filler to plump it
wholesome.
Pure honey, diluted honey, adulterated honey, are all
consumed willingly.
All with a different price tag.
Did you know most of the honey we consume is not real
honey?
40 million pounds a year this is produced.
We humans love our honey.
To the eyes of bees,
We human are bastards as honey is sweet no matter what
kind.
How pure is your humanistic honey?
How pure is your nectar of honey?

"Blooming Bastards"

Photographed: May 29, 2022
Location: Paris, France

Integration

You arrive at a new country.
You are filled with uncertainty because life in the new
country is different from back home.
Anxieties over washes you as time passes.
You still haven't found a job.
You feel unwanted because you have not been chosen for
all the 363 jobs you applied for since your arrival
You look out the window and observed the first snow fall in
your life.
You feel unwanted because you have not been chosen for
all the jobs you applied.
Hope diminishes and you feel further withdrawn.
Sinking into a tunnel of depression

Suddenly, a door of opportunity opens
To offer you an above mediocre opportunity.
The sudden realization that you are and have always been
the super NFT of your life and existence.
All the tools were in your possession.
The full integration comes from recognizing and
appreciating the most important thing: you.
Yes, you as yourself & nothing more or less
But always seeking for validation.

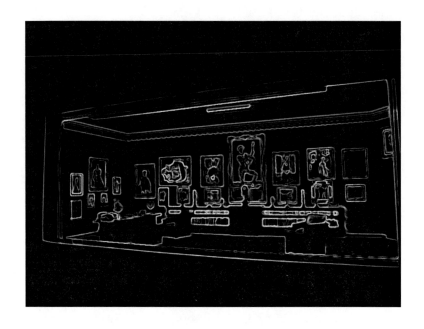

"Triple Filtered Existence"

Photographed: August 18, 2010
Location: Paris, France

Men dig their own graves

Men dig their own graves with the wrong choice(s).
You are born with all the right tools and all the options.
What you decide to pick up as your next tool, is of
significance.
Piece by piece, motion by motion, one chisels away.
In a world full of extraordinary events and lacklustre people
The sum of the equation of beings becomes the weight of
a nuclear bomb.
It hangs, but never evaporates.
Your lungs inhale it in.
You breathe it out like meditation.
Suddenly, you are back in this room.
With the same shovel to dig out or bury
Realizing now…
You have been digging your own grave all these years with
immoral choices.
How does one rest in peace and sleep at ease nightly?

"Domination"

Photographed: July 1st, 2022
Location: Seattle, WA

The Axis of Directions

So many discussions about diversity and inclusion.
How many are fully executed?
What is the real reason behind these initiatives?
When things are calm, we look for all gaps to fill the
inclusions with crazy glue.
When the Empress Corona spreads,
The crazy glue seals are rapidly removed.
Some with deliberate hesitation and some with great haste.
The East meets the West,
United by the South and North
No matter how you spin the axis of directions,
It always returns to the default axis.
One that is always the most convenient
Because the internal arrow will always point at that
direction

"Position of Pace"

Photographed: August 22, 2010
Location: Paris, France

Parasites

They are everywhere.
Whether you see it or not, they exist.
To the naked eyes, they could be your 'friend' that leeches
off you when they have urgent needs.
To the naked eyes, they could be the overly eager realtor
agent that brings you an abundance of 'good' deals,
hoping to carve the image of their face, fresh in your mind
so you can refer their services when applicable.
To the naked eyes, they could be your own siblings,
always coming to you with sob stories or manipulative
needs that affirms their lack of survivability or unwillingness
to survive and thrive.
To the naked eyes, they are also those people that come
to your home, with their self-assuming careful eyes,
scanning every single object to assess its monetary value.
Later, they use this to define a price for their services,
An extortion after the contract has ended
Just think of the movie, "Parasite."
Everything has a price tag.
To the naked eyes, they could be your very own mother
handicap to the act of gambling.
She will always call you when she is in a tight spot.
To the naked eyes, we often forget that we were all once a
parasite, safely nested in our mother's womb, sucking in all
the nutrients for development growth.
Perhaps we are all parasites of our society.
How much have you contributed to the world to make it a
better place?
Comfortably squirm and reflect on this.

"Gods & Goddesses of the Tuscan Sun"

Photographed: August 23, 2012
Location: Cinque Terre, Italy

Fear of Colors

Strange how we are all one white canvas and very
connected to the same belly button.
Strange how we all come from the same bread and butter,
but the variety has been diversified.
Strange how if there exists a form of you then there is also
a form of I.
Strange how we sometimes come together to create.
Strange how the life erupts like a calculated volcano when
there is chaos.
Strange how your melodies and mine, are kind of similar.
Strange how this same canvas can still be painted, over
and over again.

"Everyone's Canvas"

Sketched: August 23rd, 2010
Location: Cinque Terre, Italy

Eliminations

By selection this occurs.
How many times have you changed your mind today?
How many times have you made commitments that you
can't keep?
How many times have you made promises but either under
delivered or never delivered?
Are you as real as your Instagram posts?
Is it really who you are or just who you think you are?
Or is it who you pretend to be?
The irony of life lies in that perhaps everything is part of an
elimination game.
Yet, you thought you were constantly being present

"You are Eliminated"

Photographed: August 7, 2017
Location: New Orleans, USA

Dandelion

We are alone, generally speaking.
Our bodies exist individually and have been so since our
birth.
We come together esoterically throughout life continuously
finding other similar beings to connect.
Converse using the same dictionary
When a global pandemic strikes,
We become just like a dandelion, floating away.
While floating into the thinness of air, each stem continues
to detach and flutter away.
We become absorbed into the universe again.
Once again, recycled.
A new life cycle repeats again.

"Blow This"

Photographed: July 1, 2019
Location: Steveston, Richmond, BC

The Saddest Thing You can do to Your Uterus

The womb, they call it.
The space where a child is conceived.
This is a sacred space that a woman is born with.
Sometimes it is used and sometimes it is not.
The river flows in and leaves a pebble.
The river flows out and the pebble leaves.
This is again, the sacred space of your womb.
You can choose to fill it up and deliver something you create if it all works out.
Sometimes, some of us make choices like trapping a relationship.
Only then to find out, this does not lead to a fulfilled marriage or life.
Perhaps no one knows she did this on purpose but for sure they speculated it behind the curtains.
In unfortunate times, a womb becomes filled with an unwanted baggage by force
It may leave behind a child without a father and or mother
It may leave behind a child with an abandoned father and or mother
A lifetime of scars and trauma
With no choice in this
The saddest thing you can do to your uterus is to fill it with something for the sake of sustaining an unnatural yet natural situation.
And here you are…
 Is this what you wanted?
Did you have a choice in this, and can you have a choice?

"Shipping & Receiving"

Photographed: August 27, 2010
Location: Nice, France

Memories

They come strongest at night,
Usually when I am in the shower.
Replaying like scenes of an old film
A sudden intense pull,
Like a magnet pulling you into a swirling abyss.
A space specific to that memory.
The very memory of my father,
I hear his voice and his laughter.
The last time I heard and saw this was back in 2002.
He passed away in 2004.
I hear his voice asking questions about his business, a
conversation with someone else.
I hear him chuckling away to the response of another.
I saw how his smile crinkled up at the corner of his mouth.
He then mutters to himself while shaking his head slightly
about the economic downturn.
That was the year 2003.
I pulled out the voice recorder and played "dad message
1".
I pushed play to listen to "dad message 2".
Then, with the final gathering of my strength and courage,
I pushed play to listen to "dad message 3".
Today is January 11, 2020.
I haven't heard his voice since 2004.
Fast forward 16 years
Dad sounded just like I had remembered.
My cheeks wet with release of suppressed tears
My lips tasted salty.
Why are tears salty?
One must gather strength to visit their memories
Listening to what was once so familiar
Even if it means being 16 years too late.

"Life is an Infinite 8"

Still Image from my short film, Infinite 8
(2020)
Short Film: January 2020
Location: North Vancouver, BC, Canada

What the Dog Saw Everyday

Here in the city, the dog often awaits for his owner's return. In a city town home, this dog sits and watches all the daily passerby.

He saw an old lady struggling with all her strength to hull two heavy grocery bags.

He saw a pair of lovers quarrelling in front of sidewalk.

He saw a dad pushing a baby stroller while walking another big black furry dog.

He saw a young gay couple strutting in synchronized modern Charlie Chaplin outfits

He saw three white cars, two black cars, one silver car, and one Ducati bike parked in front.

He saw a little boy ride his bicycle without care and with a lot of joy.

Kind of like the joy one can observe from the movie "Billy Elliot."

A whole entire family of four then walked by.

He saw a man walked by and littered an empty coffee cup right by the tree in front.

He saw a 2020 mini cooper bumped into the 1978 911SC Porsche.

The driver got out quickly to look around, finally stopping his gaze and locking eyes with the dog before quickly getting into the car to leave.

He saw a man pick his nose.

He saw a little girl pick her nose and then examining the booger.

He saw all sorts of people walking by.

His owner finally comes home, and the dog is overcome with immense joy.

He saw a lot today…as he wagged his tail to express this. A lick!

He saw a lot of people today and they were all the same colors to him.

To his eyes, they were all one color.

He licks his owners face with affection.

Never once knowing his owner is legally blind.

All dogs see less colors than humans.

All affections are interpreted the same in their language of love.

If only he could tell you what he saw every single day.

"What the Dog Saw Everyday"

Art by Traei: Summer, 2021
Location: Vancouver, BC

"What the Real Dog Saw Everyday"

Photographed: Summer, 2010
Location: Stray dogs from the City of
Pompeii, Italy

Mothers

They are there to nurture you and give you the supposed right lessons of life.
You look up to them when you were a young child.
As you got to know things over the years, you begin to look towards others.
You learn things that your mother could not teach you through your friends.
Conflicts occur over the years and some things are never expressed appropriately.
The day came when you became a mother.
As you grapple with the challenges of being a mother, you pause.
You reflect on all the things and words said and unsaid.
As you peer into the eyes of your child, you suddenly realize that you are a reflection of your mother all along.
A reflection of all the women in your family lineage.
What you teach and give to your child will ultimately shape their future of reality.
Consider everything before taking action
So that you can change history today with each and every motion..

"Gazing"

Photographed: Summer, 2017
Location: Madrid, Spain

Polar Denning

Life is like a constant polar bear denning,
We pick up speed of pacing in the spring
We then restart during fall.
We work hard to ensure we have a safe and warm place in
the winter.

The polar bears stay in those dens to keep warm and safe
to ensure safety of the birth of their cub.
We stay in our dens at days end,
To be sheltered from the world's troubles
And to recover from the harshness of reality.

The polar bears emerge from their den when they are
ready to hunt for food.
We emerge from our den to go line up at the grocery store,
social distancing when in a pandemic.

They wait purposely until food is obtained through skillful
hunting.
We wait patiently in line at the store to get essential
groceries.

They return to the safeness of their den.
We return to the safety of whatever we define as homes.

They cuddle with their cubs and distribute food.
We look at our mobile phones and see what's happening
to other people's lives on social media.

Reset and repeat.

"Checkered Safety"

Photographed: August 23, 2010
Location: A Fabric Shoppe in Rome, Italy

People Are Strange

They make a significant effort to meet someone, only to be perhaps disappointed.
They then make another effort to speak again in better amended terms.
Yet, rushing through their emotions is the baggage they are constantly accumulating.
They release emotions not yet digested into the next sentence they shared.
In turn, launching a personal attack on the other person with a lasting impact.
Time passes without gap
Life goes on and reconciliation or not
A state of limbo prevails
More time passes and reflecting back,
One realizes that it was their egotistical and emotional struggles that allowed those piercing words to dart out from the tip of their tongues.
Slicing the other person like a paper shredding machine.
Those uttered vocal words rippling through the delicate fabric of their deliberately cherished relations
Sometimes in life, this fabric of quilt can be sewn together back into one like a mosaic.
To get there, it requires reflection and digestion,
Most importantly, self-awareness to change.
Once the self improves,
The previous lens of perception predisposed,
Becoming disposed for the purpose of recycling,
Suddenly, seeing the situation in a different light.
People are indeed strange.
We often travel far and wide to only notice what we could not relate to before,
Never connecting with what has been staring us in the eye.
People are strange.

""*Pour lui, l'amour...*"

Photographed: Summer, 2010
Location: Subway in Paris, France

Lightness

It can take many years before one reaches the lightness of
being.
It can sometimes take a decade to walk the full path of a
situation.
A marriage can last for many decades and only to be
understood finally in the first decade in separation.
What bothered you while you were growing up becomes
obsolete with time.
The youth and vitality slowly vacating your body as you
age.
Suddenly, the slowness of time encounters its first
thorough appreciation.
As you near the end of a life cycle, the lightness of our
being becomes light as clouds.
Gratitude or not,
You realize then again, this too shall pass.

"Cinque Terre"

Photographed: August, 2010
Location: Cinque Terre, Italy

The Sharpest Weapon

The sharpest weapon is not a knife.
Nor is it a sword.
The sharpest weapon is one that remains dust free, even
when not in use.
The sharpest weapon is always moist with mineralization.
The sharpest weapon is one that carries the iridescent
glow which creates ripples of changes when it is used.
The sharpest weapon may not always be used as
sometimes it is most powerful when it stands still without a
fuss.
The sharpest weapon is at times golden when it is standing
still.
How does the sharpest weapon remain so sharp you say?
Exactly from the many words that orbit off your tongue.
A muscle that never fully rests
The sharpest weapon is that you're nothing more than
what is in the mouth: the tongue of intensity.

"Sharp Memories"

Photographed: August 2010
Location: Cinque Terre, Italy

I Suffer Fools Gladly

They exist everywhere.
Day in and day out.
They are our friends, colleagues, and families.
They are strangers we see outside our homes.
The world is full of them.
They do not have the patience and see setbacks
everywhere.
They have no vision and neither the patience to cultivate
what they have sown.
The impatience in seeing quick results.
The inability to see beyond the bridge of their noses.
The constant agility to change like the wind
With no real sense of direction.
Yes, they are everywhere.
The mind is like a compass which guides the direction in
which we go.
If we follow the tremendous narrow mindedness of these
fools,
Surely, we are headed towards a life of dependency on
others.
Being self-reliant is of utmost importance.
Indulge or not indulge in their childishness,
Remember to detach, detach, and detach from the core of
your existence.

"Will They All Remember You?

Photographed: May 29, 2022
Location: A club in Paris, France

The Man That Doesn't Know How to Say No

When his friends calls, he always picks up.
Even when it is a private call, and he fears that it could be
his crazy ex
He picks up the phone with apprehension
He doesn't know how to say no.

When asked to attend a birthday party of a girl he met last
year but can't even remember the date of her birthday
He accepts the invitation and goes to the party
All for what
The fear of being alone, existing alone
#FOMO
He doesn't know how to say no

His friends laugh at him for not drinking more
Out of peer pressure and fear of missing out
He quickly reaches for another glass
Because he doesn't know how to say no

Seated behind his vehicle, he feels compelled to speed up
because his friends are following close behind
If he drives slowly, he will not be able to catch up
If he drives slowly, they will all think he is weak
If he drives poorly, the girl beside him will think less of him
He doesn't know how to say no

Fast-forward 20 years
The song "It Was a Very Good Year" by Frank Sinatra
plays in the background
He slumps on his bed and reflects…
"But now the days are short
I'm in the autumn of the year
And now I think of my life as vintage wine

From fine old kegs
From the brim to the dregs
It poured sweet and clear
It was a very good year" – Frank Sinatra

Were they all really good years?
Or was it because he didn't know how to say no.

His phone vibrates with a notification
He glances up to the sterile white ceiling and walls
His breaths, strenuous but he cannot stop thinking about
who it might be
He still doesn't know how to say no, even when he lays
dying in his lonely hospital bed.

"Maybe I Should Have Said No"

Photographed: August 30, 2018
Location: A Naked Man, USA

Homes

A home is your sanctuary.
It is a place of peace
It is a place to rest your heart, mind, and soul
It is a home of great shelter because you can find peace
even in your solitude
A home can be shared with your family
Documenting the journey of life
From your first home to your first child
When your child graduates and moves out
All the struggles and joys contained in the frame of your
home
When it's time to downsize and your children moves out
This very home has more stories and secrets to tell
An intensive narrative of events locked away
Homes, they are and should be our most cherished
sanctuary.
No matter where it is and what it is
A home is a place where one feels safe.
You decide on all the where, how, and what of that home
That is what a they call a home
A place where you can be at total peace and ease.
Wherever that is
Your home is your ultimate sanctuary.

"La Maison"

Photographed: August 24, 2010
Location: Rome, Italy

Androgynous with Audacity

She carries it close to her heart daily.
The weight of it like a large watermelon.
A black box constantly capturing what is going on lately
Every corner she turns, she snaps a quick shot
A look down inside a public garbage can, the shutter clicks!
A look in the back alley full of life's mess, the shutter clicks!
A look at the window crack on a hot summer's afternoon,
the shutter clicks!
A look at the man folding his laundry, the shutter clicks!
The man looks up as she coughs to mask the shutter
sounds
People on the streets stare at her with contempt
A woman should not be out with a strange box capturing
life
Oblivious to the looks of society
She enters the hotel lobby and frames her camera around
a lipstick-stained cup
She ponders about the story of the woman with that
lipstick, the shutter clicks!
The scent of tobacco drifts into the area
Her nose curls up and follows it down the lobby only to
realise she just missed the owner of the cigarette
She sits in the leather armchair, the seat still warm from
her body heat, shutter clicks!
She looks outside the window and decides to take a stroll
by the seaside
People are strange as they come and go
They look at her with all her camera straps and equipment
wrapped and hanging from her neck
Suddenly, she stops and looks down…
The shutter clicks.

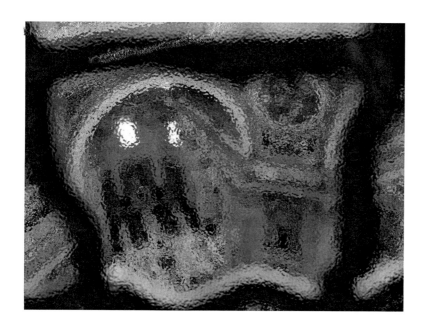

"Textured Reality"

Photographed: August 24, 2010
Location: Rome, Italy

Watching

You are looking at something now, aren't you?
"Always eyes watching you and the other voice enveloping
you. Asleep awake, indoors, or out of doors, in the bath or
bed-no escape. Nothing was your own except the few
cubic centimeters in your skull," says the Orwell in George.

We are all watching something every day.
Watching through a lens.
Watching through a screen.
Watching through texts.
Watching through memories.
Watching through history.
Watching through actions.
Watching through non-actions.
Everything watched and lost in someone else's version of
narratives.

He watches her as she watches him watching him
watching her.
What I see may not be what you see.
Take a sip.
Perhaps you can taste the people from a distance...
Tell me the texture, if you please.
I'll listen quietly.

"Listening by Watching"

Photographed: August 18, 2010
Location: A house in France.

I am the Wife of Me

Day in and day out.
She is here.
Sometimes others come but they always leave.
Even her child leaves the nest and builds their own family.
They come visit and they share a laughter with her.
But then they are gone again.
Perhaps a lonely existence at time but an exceptionally
reliable one she says.
Others may have a husband or partner to fix the broken
chair
She watches YouTube videos and conducts her own
repairs
The beauty is that in that journey she learned to paint and
polish wood
Further expanding the possibilities of that 'broken chair'
When it is garbage day
She runs into men at the recycling and garbage room
The only woman there.
A reminder of her independence because there is no other
than the wife of me
Married friends that are now divorced reminds her that
whether a he or she at days end,
One is reliant on the self because there is no other.
When married, she is the wife of him and her
When unmarried, she is the wife of her own self
When a separation occurs,
She looks up and sees a reflection of herself in the mirror.
The only thing that comes to mind is:
 "I have always been the wife of me."

"Stringent Eyes"

Photographed: September 16th, 2020
Location: Vancouver, BC

Land

No matter where you are, what you do, how you arrived,
who you are…. you are always on a piece of land.
Land, is where your 2 feet stands everyday
In which you were born on
On a surface of 148940000 km^2
Circumstances takes you to another location
Sometimes far and away then back
Traveling from land to land
From refugee camps to better lands in The Americas
From broken dreams to land that permits dreams to
become a reality
From a lush land of opportunities to a graveyard full of
destitute dreams
From barren flat land to landscapes of skyscrapers
Every year, if opportunities exist
One is always trying escape from one land to another land
A vacation here and there
Traveling without a real aim but to escape reality
In your youth, you scurry with agility from one plot to
another
Nomadic in your nature and never owning your own land
Thriving in the romanticism of being free-spirited
Sheltered under your aimless souls
Suddenly, no longer agile, you stop for a moment to inhale
a breath
Finally realizing, all the wander lusts left you homeless
Your once soaring untethered soul
Now indefinitely lost and filled with holes
Without a resting solace to shelter your existence (or non-
existence)
One is fraught with intense longing for the very land they
first opened their eyes to
You explore every potential possibility in your mind,

A physicality review to see how you can possibly \s that home again
Yet, never arriving.
Land, is where you begin and also where you end
The final destination has always been your first home.

"Where is your Castle?"

Photographed: May 27, 2022
Location: Mont Saint-Michel, UNESCO Site, France

Prince Edward Island

Surreal Childhood dreams we all once had
Flying dogs in the skies with floating red balloons
Carefree dog days in the dunes
Ocean breezes with the fresh sea air
Clouds like floating marshmallows in the skies
The sounds of crickets at night everywhere
Gazing into the warm sun surrounded by colorful butterflies
All the dogs of my childhood happily lounging around
Every person in town is without a frown
You watch the wind ripple through the tall grass
The mind becomes at ease with peace and stillness
A sense of ease washes over you
Resting in the state of nothingness
A girl with a red balloon stares out at the sea as she slowly releases it into the air
It's Anne in her green gable!

"For Two"

Photographed: September 17, 2022
Location: Steveston, BC

Showers

A comforting moment you have completely to yourself.
Naked, and in the comfort of your skin
After you lock the door,
A safety of absolute rests in that sacred space and
moment
Nobody can touch you.
Even if others wanted to use the washroom
No matter what, you are excused
As you have already claimed this territory
They will give you an apology because they've interrupted
your private affair
As you turn on the shower
Cool water pours out
It slowly becomes warm, and the temperature continues to
rise
You step into the shower
The steam rises up to the ceiling
The dampness of the shower and the hot water running
Filling your nostrils and awakening your every pore
The say the steam relaxes you
So true!
This is the most magical time of the day
Where you either separate the day from the night or the
night from the day
While in that magical moment
Your mind rolls like a camera playing out a movie
A film of all your thoughts, ideas, creativity, and mindful
harmony
Why, you ask?
Because it is in this special and magical hour and space
that no one can interrupt your thoughts
Not a voice,
Not a glowing screen,

Not someone else's narrative
Not another movie or show not worth seeing
But purely, your own voice in your head
Situated in the safety of your shower of sanctuary
That, is why showers are so special
So, go take a shower now.

"A Tethered Liberty"

Photographed: July 8, 2022
Location: Vancouver, BC

The Artifacts of Life

Sometimes in life, every object isn't always just material
They may appear as material and tangible
But I see them as artifacts
We are living museums, constantly collecting.
Every piece of object we come across is fascinating
because it is a part of history.
An artifact of life.
Hence, why when we visit museums we become so
fascinated by each piece of object
Not one was really part of an accidental collection
Each piece had a where, when, what, why and how…
As life continues…
Archive, archive, and more archive.
Expanding in this big museum of 'me.'

"Miniature Reality"

Photographed: September 26 2022
Location: Public Space, Mont eal, CA

Astigmatism

If only you knew what this was
Something to do with the way you see
Something to do with the way you shape things
Something to do with the image in front of you
Visions
You think you see what they see
But in truth all is not what it appears to be
And no one ever sees the same
Astigmatism is such a thing, a condition in which the eyes
does not focus light
Sometimes things are too blurry, distorted, and bright
At any distance, it can cause you eyestrain, headaches
and troubles driving at night
The worst of astigmatism is when your tears stream down
your face
While driving alone in a dark night
Where all the streetlights reflect back the glare
Sorrows reflected in those eyes that does not focus light
Life becomes a milky glare
Halos of glitter
So, this is astigmatism
Leading you to your starry starry night
As Vincent said

"Starry Station"

Photographed: August 19, 2010
Location: Nice, Franc

Doubts

Every being in this universe has experienced doubt
Whether you are just doing your thing
Doubt is everywhere
The lesson of doubt comes from different life experiences
You see a great deal and you are filled with doubts

Remembering the last time
You did not notice the fine print
You recklessly fell in love with her thinking she was
everything you've ever dreamed of
Later to realize she was a reflection of another copy of the
original

He was prince charming that swept you off your feet in
spring
Then summer came and she called herself his girlfriend
Winter became full of doubts
Finally wrapping up with an ending
A full cycle repeating in spring again

Someone offered you a shot to drink
Telling you it was delicious
You trusted this so-called friend and downed the shot
Only to find out it was a Sambuca not a Slippery Nipple

Your dog shits everywhere because she got mad you
didn't bring her out
You kneel down with your assuring praise to coax her over
to her pile of shit
When she comes finally, you scold her in this training
opportunity
Even she has lost trust in you the next time you call her to
the same spot

The homeless guy sits quietly in the rain by the back alley
You approach kindly with a sandwich in hand
He looks you up and down and studies every inch of the
sandwich
He remembers the last time he got beat up for food
This sandwich will not provide the satisfaction of a high
that money can buy
His doubts are real and full of circumstantial fear
He shakes his head and declines the sandwich

Doubts, they exist everywhere
In your every waking moment

"A Sunny Rainy Day"

Photographed: June 19th, 2022
Location: Robson Street, Vancouver, BC.

Tolerance

When you have a bad day
You kick and scream like a child
He holds you and tells you he loves you
When he smothers you with love
You run away from his stranglehold
Along the way, you throw a lighter at him
Instead of yelling back he tells you
That he loves you no matter what
He knows it is one of your tantrums
He takes the lighter and lights up a candle
When he is away
The mind calms down
You regret the things you've said
Then reflected on the how and whys
When you can no longer find excuses for your self
You slowly and sheepishly apologize
For all the childish misbehaviours
He accepts it all and instead of scolding you
He strokes your hair and tells you he loves you
Your eyes filled with tears
This, is your soul mate
Your tantrum came because of your high expectations
And past disappointments
He already saw and anticipated this with the cushion of
tolerance
Because he knew you were going through some stuff

"I forgive you."

Photographed: August 17, 2010
Location: Seine River, France

Eulogy Part 1

Here lies Bob
Always full of muted thoughts and conservations
Mostly quiet at social gatherings
Nothing interesting to say
The words that come out are like gentle pastel colored
poetry
Beautiful yet insignificant
Not a conversationalist at heart
And a true sheep of life
On his last day
Some may remember him but what is certain is everyone
will forget this sheep

Eulogy Part 2

Here lies Jones
Always full of witty thoughts and speech
No saliva has ever been wasted
Things expressed were originals that always captivates a
real audience
People actually listened with interest
Stories and thoughts
Highly entertaining which made people think…." I never
thought of that!"
Bold and loud were his words
Never a dull moment
He led the sheep rather than lived sheepishly
Though his words were sometimes abrasive, raw, and
sarcastic
Never gentle nor poetic
When he died, all will remember, and he is never forgotten.
The irony of life is apparent in these eulogies
Which one best describes you?

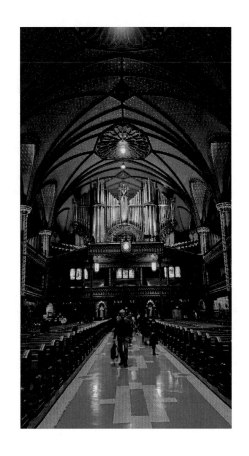

"The Beginning & End"

Photographed: September 26, 2022
Location: Montréal, BC

The Sun

The storm and wind yesterday brought the barometric pressure of a migraine
Today the sun came out after a day of heavy rain and strong winds
Releasing 384.6 yotta watts of energy
Radiating over the area of a sphere with the radius of approximately 93,000,000 miles
This changes everything
No matter what the mood was sombre about yesterday
Today the sky is bright
You can play with the cast of shadows on your face
Looking left and looking right
How it contrasts the contours of your face
Yes, it is a thing
When the sun comes out
Everyone longs to go outside
Even the ones that exits the home with contempt
They eagerly put on their coat, hat, and mask
Out they go into the bright sunlight
Soak it in!
A sense of freedom and liberation
Your migraine is suddenly gone
In that moment your worries are on hold
Nothing can touch you really at this moment
A pigeon suddenly flies over to salute to your positivity
It does not shy away from the click of your camera
You look it in the eye and it salutes you with its eyes
It then flaps away happily into the beautiful blue sky
Filled with revived energy from head to toe
A full reset to take on the rest of this beautiful day
That, is the power of the sun

Mantras of Happiness

Whatever religion you have
Wherever you are
Even if you are an atheist
There exist a mantra of happiness
It comes in all languages and format
Be ready to embrace it
When it is heading your way at full speed
Remember to open that universal door and welcome it in

"The Koi Mantra"

Art by Traei Tsai: 2019-2020
The Koi Mantra (Oil on Canvas)
Vancouver, BC

Elastic Heart 🖤

A circumference of 0.5 cm to 15.5 cm
Contained within the rhythm of beats beneath our chest
It shrinks and expands
Just like an elastic balloon
Every day we encounter things
Sometimes muted and sometimes rapidly like an artistic vengeance
Racing with excitement like the violin strings in the songs of four seasons
After a heartbreak
A life shattering experience
Your heart feels like glued broken glass
As each beat expands
You can feel the crackling of the glass
Pieces chipping and flaking away
You pop an aspirin to numb the pain of these cuts
Longing for the day your heart becomes filled with lacquered formaldehyde
Sleep befalls you
Permitting the much-needed rest
You awake the next day
To your dog licking your face
A sense of gratitude fills your beating heart
You marvel at the elastic capacity of this heart
Always forbearing and enduring beyond your default strength

What an amazing elastic heart! 🖤

"Forgotten Elastic Heart"

Photographed: August 5, 2022
Location: Undisclosed

Empathy

Oh! It means compassion
Oh! It means feeling sorry for another
Oh! It means handling situations with caution

Does one really understand empathy?
The real question is do you need to understand empathy?
So many world leaders lack empathy while many fall under
their protection
Some are excellent and some are terrible
Some care about people and some only after careful
selection
Empathy to me is relating to another human being
Like how your dog relates to you emotionally without words
It's how she licks your face because she knew your father
passed away before you did
She knows you didn't like to be licked in the face
But she mops your tear-stained face with loving licks
Empathy is when your partner correctly assume your
emotions
Even though you thought it was all well hidden
They saw right through your internal commotion
Every day there is an opportunity for empathy
Every day there is an opportunity for compassion
Yet, there is no compassion without empathy
Vice versa
So, if you have wondered the whys of their lack of empathy
It is ultimately also a lack of compassion

"Pete Was Here"

Photographed: May 26, 2022
Location: Paris, France

Let Go

To commence
You accept
You then immerse
Just a bit longer to the familiar
Before slowly letting go
Like holding a fish between your palms
It wriggles in the grasp of your hands
Before it dashes out like a motorboat
Escaping from your slippery grip
Some people came and stayed in your life
They brought you happiness and great heartaches
They even allow others to come shatter your hopes
Then they runaway like a cowardly puss
Never able to muster the courage to speak
Every so often they trouble you with words
Attacking only through texts
These words became constant threats
The restless souls of unease
Never ceasing to pass their frustrations to you
With hopes you'd crumble apart
Like an old hard cookie
Pieces of you
Pieces of you
Are just crumbs of a once uniformed existence?
When it falls apart
There will be no more resistance
Sometimes, you just have to let it all go

"Where is your temple?"

Photographed: August 26, 2018
Location: Washington, DC

Resistance

Imagine a pull against your will
Imagine going to the right when you really want to go left
Imagine going forward but all you want to do is stand still
Imagine extracting yourself by force
When you really want to just rest
Imagine when the whole world wants you to fail
And you just want to be heard
Imagine wanting to rid yourself of something
But it just does not want to go
Imagine wishing for dreamless sleeps
Only to wake up from nightmares
When all the odds are against you
You charge ahead in full force because there is no other way
And so, you begin another 24 hours in this brand-new day
Resisting resistance

"Invisible Ballerina"

Photographed: August 17, 2010
Location: Paris, France

Racists

Some things do not change
Hidden well under its charitable campaigns
No one knows the deep dark secrets
Of its unconscious bias
Don't we all have this?
Such visible racial tolerance the world provides
A price tag hangs on her neck
Because of her yellow skin
Being Chinese has everything to do with it in 1885
One by one they landed
Cha-ching!
The head of state is rich with today's $1.5 Billion dollars
from this
A slave to my ethnicity
Chained to my origin on this foreign land
Because I am Chinese, they will not hire me
I will forgive but I will never ever forget
Why did you call me an Alien on that passport?
Resiliency and tenacity has always been in our blood
Fighting against the currents in a world where we are not a
majority but a visible minority
Racism today is better than the head tax in 1885
But it is everywhere
It never went away
Just because we are quiet and polite
Shying away from opportunities of spotlight
Our sufferings and struggles are real
To unveil this unconscious bias
It requires you to remove your filtered lenses
And cut all the ghostly head tax price tags
When will we cut all the strings of racism?

"Everything is For Sale"

Photographed: August 26, 2018
Location: Washington, USA

Gratitude of the Common Girl

She turns on the TV and clicks the next button
Scrolling through new episodes of different shows
On the narratives and realities of others

Her phone vibrates
She checks how many likes she received for her post
about the new bag she got
Her heart sinks due to the lack of likes
Filled with disappointment
She gets up and walks to the bathroom
Turning on the light she sees her own reflection
Noticing her fake lashes needs to be refilled
She messages the girl that does lash refills at home
Setting up the next available appointment
She can now rest and look forward to a new set of plush
artificial lashes
Allowing her to bat them at the next party

While washing her face the next morning
She notices her nail polish was chipped
Without hesitation she books the next appointment for her
nails
Filled with gratitude
She sighs with a sense of relief

It's Friday and she has a party to go to
Standing in front of her closet
Glancing from left to right
She decides there is nothing to wear
She quickly gets dressed and heads out to go shopping
Tapping her plastic card
With a mental note that she will pay with her next pay
cheque

With the new outfit now laid out on her bed
She showers and starts layering on her mask
Contour this and contours that
After 20 minutes her face shape is completely different
from birth
Eye shadows of caramel cream tones
Intense eyeliner that does not smudge
She decides to put on fake lashes in between
appointments
Curl, curl, curl….
Brush, brush, brush
Layer by layer she thickens her lashes
Blush, bronze, powder, and set
She smacks her lips together for that perfect pout
She is ready for the party
Damn! I look good!

Arriving fashionably late
She picks up a glass of wine
Never fond of the taste but drinks it to fit in
The clock ticks and she is on her 4th glass of wine
Flirtatious conversations with this man turns out to be a
hollow pursuit
As his wife suddenly surprises with a visit
Feeling tipsy she catches an Uber home
Sobering up with a cup of hot honey lemon Chamomile tea
She curls up on her sofa and scrolls through new episodes
Shows of glamorous irrelevant realities
Her favorite reality shows has a new season
She suddenly sobers up and plays the 1st episode
Watching intently with envy and intense longing

If she loved her life so much
Why does she ache to watch those shows to drown in
other people's narratives?

"Inner Reflection"

Photographed: November 16, 2019
Location: Vancouver, BC, Canada

The Vulnerabilities of Love

You crave it when you don't have it
Then it comes
A phase of honeyed existence
Followed by rollercoaster ups and downs
If there were no obstacles of resistance
We tend to create one so that we can drown within the so-
called definition of love
What is love anyways?
Is love what society defines for you?
Is love what is defined in the dictionaries?
Is love exactly what those dead poets and authors have
coined?
Is love what your religion tells you?
Is love what social media presents to you?
Is love what your mother, father, brother, or sister tells
you?
Is love what your significant other purrs to you?
Is love really what you think it is yourself or is it a love that
belongs to the definition of everything else?

"Yes, or No?"

Photographed: May 2019
Location: Cannes, France

A Blender of Love – The Magic Bullet of Love

Perhaps love is a bit of everything like a blended and not
so smooth smoothie
When you finally take a chance
It is immediately happy and liberating
Followed by discontent and a lack of appreciation
Being taken for granted
One forgets what it means to treasure love as is
It then feels like your heart has been dropped into the
blender
Only this time you come out smashed and chopped
Time passes and you heal
And repeat.
Your mended broken heart gets dropped into the blender
again…
So blended that you forget which ones were the original
pieces and which ones were the newer pieces
The mended broken heart version 2 begins a new journey
and repeats until completely defeated
Are you currently loving with your fusioned heart?
Do they also love you for who you are with your blended
heart?

"Inner Connection"

Photographed: August 26, 2018
Location: Public Space in Chicago, USA

Short Cuts

He is always cutting corners
When confronted, he deflects and lies
Sometimes he gets away and sometimes not
When he dodges a bullet,
He is extra proud with ego
When he gets caught
His thick alligator skin protects him like Gore-Tex to rain
Shameless!
They all called out.
But he shrugs and walks on.

"It's All Staged"

Photographed: July 2017
Location: South Bank, London

What is love?

Love is a feeling
Love consists of multiple actions
I have loved because I was loved but perhaps never in
love because of some lack of love
What is love you say?
With all the definitions of love globally, not one is the
ultimate love.
Persians have layers of love
Asians have layers of love
Italians have layers of love
Brazilians have layers of love
Japanese have layers of love
Taiwanese have layers of love
Chinese have layers of love
Europeans have layers of love
One is expressive and one is not
But it does not ever mean less love
Love is of different capacities and can be of many different
kinds

Maybe…
Instead of pondering and forgetting the doing
Put your focus on love and not what its definition should be

"What is Love?"

Photographed: July 18, 2017
Location: Somewhere in the gaps of Spain

Peace within the Self

How does one find this?
After going through tribulations of trials and errors
One arrives in distraught
Not seeing but seeing clearly of the self in the mirror
Searching for an anchor while filled with complete
overwrought
Like a wounded bird resting on a half-broken branch
A very unsteady perch
Pausing momentarily in this fleeting life
Examining the existence of our dilapidated and isolated
stanch
Without peace and just rife
Suddenly the chirping of crickets over washes with
calmness
We find peace within the self,
To ultimately liberate oneself.

"I Stand in Peace"

Photographed: May 24, 2022
Location: Eze, France

Comforting Sounds

It's not easy being a woman
Despite these comforting sounds we hear
She tells him she cannot see the light
He embraces her and tells her it is all right
She trembles under the security of his arms
Temporarily alleviating all life's harms
Despite the storming weather outside
All has become the comforting sounds of the rain
When the moment passes
No longer in those arms
Reality overtakes those comforting sounds
Suddenly she is alone
He has left

Perhaps silence has always been the best comforting
sounds all along

"Comforting Love"

Photographed: August 17, 2010
Location: Seine River, France

Advil for the ♥

When you are down
Take an Advil
To numb your ♥
Without the side effects like other drugs
There is no highs and lows
Just a muting of sensations
Not feeling the deep cut in your ♥
Even if you poured alcohol on that open wound
The pain is quite diluted
As it passes through your system
You flush it down the toilet
When the pain returns
Go swallow another Advil
Repeat when necessary
Keep swallowing those Advil's until you are better
When it can no longer numb your pain
Perhaps it is time to upgrade to a stainless-steel heart

"Unwanted"

Photographed: June 24, 2012
Location: Vancouver, BC

Black Swan

Belonging to where we don't belong
We are all Black swans, aren't we?
Inappropriately rationalized after the fact
With questionable blind insight
Dark and mysterious
Craving for anonymity among the white swans
Nomadically gliding across the purifying waters
To reach the glistening white sands
Soaking up those dark feathers
Hoping to bleach our nature
Coming to a delightful disappointment
Discovering with sudden inspiration
We are so incredibly special after all
In our original essence of existence
The black swan always stands strong and true
Independently
Alone

"You are your own Emergency Exit"

Photographed: July 2017
Location: Barcelona, Spain

A lot of us

Will never know what it is like
To have a permanent home
A forever home is what they called
Where you can park your bike outside
And never have it stolen
Because gone are those easy times
Of assurance and ease
With a sprinkle of peace

A lot of us
Will never know what it is like
To always know if you have nowhere to go
There is somewhere to stay
To rest your head there
Where the door opens wide when you arrive

A lot of us
Are renters living in a city that we can't afford
Somehow it is the norm
Accepted by a lack of form
Because there is nothing else you can do

A lot of us
Live day to day
In easily interpreted settings
Digest food that looks good on Instagram
Sharing with others publicly
But only to crawl into a small bed
In the corner that the selfie camera never sees

A lot of us
Pretend that it is ok
Perhaps even accept as reality

And think that this daily grind
Is great when there is a measurable outcome

A lot of us
Gravitates towards what is easy to accept
To fulfil the hollow loneliness, we feel
By whatever brand of glue, we can find
So that the layers of onion will never have to be peeled

A lot of us
Will share stories and pictures
Like everyone else
Bragging about the repeated things, events, and places
Living mostly in memories
Instead of being present

A lot of us
Will mostly live this way, till the end of life
Not knowing a burial plot cost $35000 just for land
Based on today's google search
So that one can lie there without a coffin
To rest in your eternal bed
Add another $6000

A lot of us
Live day to day
Because there is no choice
Or because it was chosen by you

A lot of us
Will never be buried in our own back yard
Because they own no true yard
This is a lot of us from the view of a little bit of them

"Where is home?"

Photographed: August 2022
Location: West Georgia Street, Vancouver
BC, Canada

Where am I going?

All the directions I want
Orbiting in a strange & conflicted frequency
The life of me and her
Where lines are blurred to semi co-exist
Week after week
Discoveries unfold without force
Complimentarily interruptive in its organic state

Humans are strange
We are strange
A strange life of existences
Pretending to be meaningful
Yet that's a life

Perhaps we are all tools
Perhaps I am truthful
Perhaps you are forgetful
Perhaps we are just a bunch of tools of the fools
Perhaps together, we can be hopeful

"Empty Station"

Photographed: August 24, 2010
Location: Rome, Italy

Rainy Day

If the weather is sunny today
You dress in t-shirt and shorts
Being present you don't plan and prep
The sunshine suggests a holiday
Sailing away in your boats
Forgetting the extra jacket and pants
The stormy clouds creeps in
When the weather turns bad
Everyone is full of rants
And forgets to reflect within
And becomes a little sad
Because life is truly Murphy's Law
While in temporary ignorant bliss
We forget to save and prep
The extra cushion for future comforts
All but one who did not dismiss
The opposite of a common sheep
He who preps rests in the laurels of the efforts of others
And not in the charity duration of a flower's bloom

Rainy Days….
They come and go

Have you prepped for all the rainy days to come?

"Finding Shelter"

Photographed: January 14, 2014
Location: Panama

The Chase

Go chase after your dreams
For dreams are what reality becomes
It's okay to top off your coffee with cream
Your dreams becomes the source of your vitality
Forming a part of your daily living
A life full of adventure continues
Unfolding to all of your choosing
Finding all possible ways to enjoy
Everything that this life will give you
The chase makes all dreams a reality.
Go chase your dreams now.

"A Field of Dreams"

Photographed: August 19, 2019
Location: Chilliwack, BC, Canada

The Small Things that Make You Sweat

Don't sweat the small stuff they say
Time always moves forward
In the end all things have happened
And somehow, they all worked out for you
A loss of nothing and a gain of many
Material happiness is short lived
Passion and dedication brings happiness
Lasting because you are living it
For the self and for others

If you don't live for yourself
How can you be there for others?
If you can't stand strong
How will you support others?

"Let's share?"

Photographed: August 2010
Location: Naples, Italy

RGSS

Root Well.
Grow Strong.
Stand Tall.
Share and spread seeds.

Master the sowing and harvesting in life
And thrive you will

"Uprooting & Crash Landing"

Photographed: September 27, 2009
Location: Oregon, WA, USA

La Nuit

J'aime la nuit
Because it is peaceful and full of solitude
A good time for deep reflections
Noone can bother you
J'aime la nuit
Even bad news mostly get delivered in the AM.
When you wake in the morning
While refreshed,
You are following everyone's schedule of a rat race
9-5 or 5-9,
Opening hours for postal delivery, banks, doctors, hair
salons, debt collectors' office and daily work
Most do not work at night
Nobody bothers you, generally.

You are free to create things in depth without external
interruptions
Liberated from societal norms of scheduled structure
You can finally be at ease.

J'adore la nuit
La nuit nous appartient
The day belongs to everyone where you must fight and
compete.
Sharing everyday with unease
Under the façade of many premium marketing images of
ease.
Yet, no one is truly at peace in the daytime.
Are you truly at ease now?

J'adore la nuit.

"Nuit"

Photographed: May 29, 2022
Location: Eiffel Tower, Paris, France

Forbearance

When two people collide and they still choose to work
things out
This is the foundation of forbearance
Full of empathy to anticipate all the how and whys
Exercising patience through challenges and obstacles
Forbearance comes through like a beacon of sunshine
Magnifying the possibilities of compassion
To unify and mend what has been conflicting
Balancing all the disharmony
Purifying the extremities to create a safe space for
forgiveness
Moving to a place of understanding and harmony
Which can weather any storm or chaos

While one does not always have to agree on everything
We are honestly different but fundamentally the same
With tolerance and kindness
Anything can be accomplished with a sense of
forbearance.

"Layered Existence"

Photographed: July 18, 2017
Location: Madrid, Spain

Fin.

Nailing You to Your Place

When things aren't right
Pick up the nail and hammer
To put it in its right place
Joining all like and similar
In this shared space
May it rest in peace
As everything is in its right place.

When the night begins, another day awaits

"Sunset"

Photographed: September 27, 2009
Location: Oregon Coast, WA

"The most important relationship you will ever have is the one you have with yourself."

- Diane Von Furstenberg –

About the Author

Traei Tsai is a Taiwanese born Canadian local writer, actress, fashion model, and painter based in Vancouver. In 2020, she was in the globe's first "Corona Movie", a dramatic thriller and the world's first feature film about Coronavirus and Xenophobia. This was featured in the New York Times, BBC, The Vancouver Sun, The Hollywood Reporter, The Guardian, The Times, Le Figaro, International Business Times, and many other news around the globe. She has also trained in modeling with Coco Rocha, in New York City.

A graduate of SFU in Social Sciences in Anthropology and Sociology. She has been involved in multiple ways in the shaping of Canadians settling in Canada. Since 2009, her career in both private and public sectors has raised continuous awareness in social issues in the realm of visible minorities in Canada. Traei is also the Vice-President of BC Minorities in Film & TV Society, a non-profit organization advocating for minorities and diversity inclusion in front and behind the camera. Her passion lies in creating layers of positive social impacts that continuously support a better community and world that we share.

Traei also paints and was nominated as the first Canadian Official Winner at MiraBan Art in London, UK for her painting, "The Koi Mantra" - a painting highlighting the strength of life, women in their vulnerability, shyness, modesty, and allure through delicate objects of the antique ceramic from the Qing Dynasty period. During the COVID19 pandemic, she has completed a new piece of art called "I dream of Sailing", which is available on SAATCHI Art.

Honest Reflections is her first book on sincere reflections on life. She is also currently working on a book called, "Her Stories Untold" (www.herstoriesuntold.com), a global book project on women empowerment, capturing true stories of women around the globe. As featured in an interview on Global News Canada on Mother's Day in 2020, she talks about how women can support other women with her stories. Her Stories Untold host live talks online featuring special guests from all walks of life. It is also available on Podcast via Spotify, Apple ITunes and so on.

She is currently pre-developing several projects in film, TV, and animation.

Made in United States
North Haven, CT
22 April 2024

51434273R00111